THE TRANS FORMERS™

MEGATRON'S FIGHT FOR POWER

written by JOHN GRANT
illustrated by MIKE COLLINS and MARK FARMER

Ladybird Books Loughborough

Spike wrote in his diary: "I wonder what the Decepticons are up to. It is more than a week since we saw any sign of them."

He put the diary away and joined his father who was working with a group of Autobots on the mammoth task of rebuilding the Autobot space cruiser. Some day, with the help of their two human friends, the Autobots hoped to return to their own planet Cybertron.

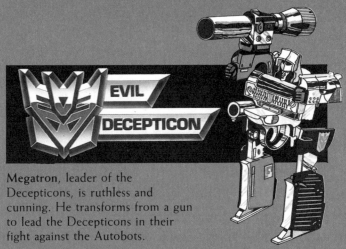

EVIL DECEPTICON

Megatron, leader of the Decepticons, is ruthless and cunning. He transforms from a gun to lead the Decepticons in their fight against the Autobots.

Soundwave transforms from a cassette recorder to a Decepticon communicator robot and acts as a radio link for the other Decepticons. He is able to read minds and will use blackmail for his own gain. Soundwave is despised by all other Decepticons.

Laserbeak is cowardly and will run for safety if he is threatened. He can fly at speeds of up to 250 mph and transforms from a spy cassette to the Decepticon interrogation robot.

Starscream transforms from a plane to the Decepticon air commander robot. He can fly faster than any of the Decepticons and seeks to replace Megatron as leader. Starscream is ruthless and cruel.

Rumble is small and tough. When he transforms from a spy cassette to the demolition robot, he transmits low frequency groundwaves to create powerful earthquakes.

Ravage likes to operate alone and is the craftiest of all Decepticons. He transforms from a spy cassette to a saboteur robot. He is very good at hiding himself in the shadows of the night and can walk without making a sound.

Once, long ago, a race of robot beings called `Autobots were forced to wage war against another race of robots called Decepticons, to bring peace back to their home planet of Cybertron.

As the war went on, chance brought both sides to Earth. They crashed so violently on landing that all the robots lay in the Earth's crust, seemingly without life, for over four million years.

Suddenly the energy set in motion by a powerful volcanic eruption gives them life once more – and the war starts all over again here on Earth. Among the robots' many strange powers is the ability to transform into other shapes, and they use this to disguise themselves to fit in with the civilisation they find on Earth. The Autobots have to defend themselves, they have to protect this planet with all its valuable resources and the people who live here – and they must also build a new space ship if they are ever to get back to Cybertron...

British Library Cataloguing in Publication Data

Grant, John, 1930-
   Megatron's fight for power.—(Transformers. Series 853; v. 2)
   I. Title II. Collins, Mike III. Farmer, Mark
   823'.914[J]   PZ7
   ISBN 0-7214-0896-6

First edition

Work on the rebuilding of their space cruiser was going well but fuel was going to be a problem. "Unless we can find a source of energy to drive it," Spike's father explained, "the cruiser will sit here for ever."

The giant shape of Optimus Prime, leader of the Autobots, loomed up. "That must never happen," he said. "We must return to Cybertron. Our duty lies in defeating the evil plans of Megatron and the Decepticons and restoring our planet to a world of peace."

In the Decepticon hide-out, Megatron raged at his followers.

"Things are going much too slowly! Our spaceship is nearing completion but our store of energon cubes is still far short of what we need!"

The Decepticons cowered at Megatron's words, that is, except Starscream. "Things are going slowly because Megatron is soft," he sneered. "The Decepticons need a *leader*, not a doddering old fool. Now if I were in charge, we would have swept this miserable planet clear of Autobots long ago. Our energon cubes would be full. And Cybertron would now be the centre of a great Galactic empire. MY EMPIRE!"

Megatron turned to Soundwave. "Send out Buzzsaw. Extend the search range. We must locate further energy sources."

Soundwave ejected the small cassette which instantly transformed into the bird-like robot, Buzzsaw. "Operation search and report," Soundwave commanded. "Radius of search, five hundred kilometres."

Buzzsaw soared into the sky on powerful mechanical wings. He circled a couple of times to get his bearings. Then he began his search pattern. His cameras recorded everything on the ground as he passed over. Infra-red and ultra-violet sensors collected information and passed it to his electronic memory banks. A mini-radar scanner searched for objects too distant for the cameras.

Buzzsaw's trip-counter steadily recorded how far he had flown. Soon it showed that he was close to the farthest limit of his mission. As he flew over the last kilometre of the search area, the radar gave a warning bleep. There was something of interest ahead. The signal grew stronger every second but that was further than his orders allowed him to go.

As he reached the edge of the search area, the mechanical bird banked sharply and sped swiftly on a return course to the Decepticon base.

Soundwave saw Buzzsaw swooping in to land. In a moment the metal bird had transformed back into a cassette. Soundwave caught the cassette in mid-air and hurried to Megatron with it.

Megatron slotted the cassette into the playback machine and adjusted the controls on the screen. They saw a picture of the land that Buzzsaw had flown over. There were woods, mountains and rivers. Sometimes there were houses and small villages. But they saw nothing that suggested a source of energy to power their inter-galactic space cruiser.

The cassette had almost run out. Megatron turned away angrily. Soundwave called him back. "Faint radar signal," he said. "Beyond limit of search." He re-adjusted the screen controls. "Advise visual inspection."

"I will investigate this personally," said Megatron. "You shall accompany me, Soundwave." In a moment they were airborne and heading for the location indicated by the radar blip.

As he watched them disappear into the distance, Starscream muttered, "Megatron is growing careless. He is foolish to go off alone except for that animated tape recorder, Soundwave. My time is near. I can feel it. Soon the Decepticons will obey *me*. Then they will know what it is to have a proper leader."

He turned and strode off. He needed his plan fully worked out ready to put into operation when his chance came.

Already far away, Soundwave's sensors began to detect something ahead and below. He swooped towards the ground. Megatron followed. The country was hilly. Beneath was a long narrow valley and through the valley ran a road. Travelling along the road was a small van.

"Autobots!" cried Megatron.

"No," said Soundwave. "Humans. Not dangerous. Advise non-interference." And the two Decepticons went on their way again.

As Megatron and Soundwave disappeared over the hills the van continued on its way up the valley. There were two men in it. "Well, Professor," said the driver, "you will soon know if your solar energy system is successful."

"I know already," replied the Professor. "It is *too* successful. The energy level is more than we can use. There is still much work to be done."

The valley was now very wide. They came to a high fence and a steel gate that barred their way. At the touch of a button in the van, the gate slid open and they passed through into the complex.

Massive pieces of machinery towered above the van as it pulled up beside a small building halfway across the valley floor. Rail-mounted steel cradles supported four huge mirrored saucers. Together, they formed a square almost a kilometre wide.

Cables and steel ducts connected them to a smaller saucer in the centre, close to the building. From the smaller saucer a broad beam of golden energy played on the shining metal surface of an enormous sphere which was poised on a tripod of slender metal legs.

Inside the building, the Professor and his assistant checked the instruments. "Perhaps we should have someone here all the time," said the assistant.

"There's no need," said the Professor. "The whole complex is completely automatic."

They left the building and drove back through the complex. The steel gates opened for them and slid shut as they passed.

The dust from the passing of the van had barely settled when there was a movement on the rim of

the valley and the sun sparkled on something
metal. Megatron and Soundwave stood on a hill-
top and looked down across the valley. Megatron
knew that they had found what they were
searching for.

"Of course!" he said, gazing at the enormous
saucers. "Energy from the sun! Magnificent! Here
we can charge all the energon cubes we need.
Send a message, Soundwave. I want the entire
Decepticon force assembled here, without delay."

At the Decepticon base, Starscream listened as Megatron's orders came over on the radio.

"Decepticons to solar complex... thirty two point five kilometres from base, on bearing two three four degrees. Assemble at building in centre of complex."

"At last!" cried Starscream. "His brain circuits have failed! He has made his last mistake in letting me know where to find him. By nightfall the mighty Megatron will be a rusting pile of scrap iron!"

He called for Rumble. "Assemble the others for
immediate action," he ordered. "Ask no questions.
Believe me when I say that this day will be
remembered in Decepticon history. You will do
exactly as I command."

"But, Megatron..."

"Megatron! Megatron! That's all I ever hear,"
shouted Starscream. "After today no one will need
to use that name again! Decepticons –
SCRAMBLE!"

Things were still peaceful at the Autobot base. Ironhide said, "I think I'll take a little trip into the hills and stretch my suspension." He transformed into his van disguise, switched on his engine and drove off into the countryside.

After a while he stopped on a low hill. "Might be something worth listening to on the radio," he said to himself. He extended his

scanner aerial from the roof of the van and slowly rotated it as he tuned the radio. "Nothing but commercials!" he muttered.

He swung the aerial once more. Then he stopped. Through the jumble of music and voices, he picked out something different. He turned up the volume then he moved the aerial again until he had a bearing on the signal.

Next moment he was driving at top speed back to base.

The Autobots rushed out as Ironhide skidded to a halt in a cloud of dust.

"DECEPTICONS!" he shouted. "Moving fast and airborne! I picked up their signals!"

"See what you can find, Hound," said Optimus Prime. Hound activated his radar scanner and infra-red detector. They listened to a distant mutter of radio signals. "They're moving away," said Optimus Prime. "According to Ironhide's bearing they are headed for the desert. What can they want there?"

"The only thing I've heard of is some sort of Government research laboratory. Perhaps they plan to pay it a visit," said Spike.

"One thing's for sure," said Ironhide. "They're not going to arrive with a box of chocolates!"

"Well, we haven't been invited to the party," said Optimus Prime. "But I think we should take a look. I'll investigate with our two human friends. Jazz, be ready to despatch a strike force at a moment's notice. I'll keep in touch by radio."

Quickly, Optimus Prime transformed into his truck disguise. Spike and his father climbed into the cab. "I never thought that I'd be a trucker," said Spike.

"Neither did I," replied his father, "particularly in a truck that can talk to you while you ride in it!"

"All set?" said Optimus Prime. "Here we go."

The huge articulated truck moved forward and gathered speed as it rumbled towards the distant solar research station.

Meanwhile, Starscream led the Decepticons swiftly over the hills towards the valley where Megatron and Soundwave waited impatiently. A light flashed on Soundwave's chest pack. "Decepticons within low-frequency detector range," he reported.

"Right," said Megatron. "That gives us just enough time to prepare."

Over the rim of the hills, came the airborne Decepticons. Below lay the solar complex. And in the centre was the building where Megatron and Soundwave were to meet them.

Starscream laughed as they swooped closer.

"Stand by," he ordered. "I want the entire force on the ground at the same time. Each Decepticon will take up his position according to *my* orders. Fire on my command!"

In a final rush, the Decepticons dropped to the ground and quickly surrounded the building. There were no windows: only one metal door. They trained their weapons on the door and waited silently.

Then Starscream stepped forward. "Come out, Megatron!" he shouted. "Your reign is over. If you act sensibly I might even be merciful!"

From the shadow of one of the giant solar saucers came a flash and the roar of a fusion-cannon. The charge ripped a long furrow in the ground beside Starscream who was hurled off his feet by the blast. His smoking weapon still pointed at his fallen rival, Megatron stepped forward, followed by Soundwave.

"So you are prepared to be merciful, Starscream?" he said. "You will *never* make a Decepticon leader. Decepticon leaders do not show mercy. They are ruthless. They are also cunning. Did you really think that I would sit alone to await your pleasure?"

Starscream grovelled in the dirt. "Spare me, Megatron," he begged.

"I will spare you this time," said Megatron. "But not because I am merciful. A Decepticon leader must be practical and I need every pair of hands if we are ever to reactivate the space cruiser and return to Cybertron. Beware the day when you are of no further use to me."

Megatron turned to Soundwave. "Prepare the energon cubes," he ordered.

Optimus Prime stopped on the crest of a hill.
Below in the valley a road wound its way into the
distance. Spike climbed down from the cab. "That
should take us in the right direction," he said.
They joined the road and a few minutes later they
had reached the complex. Spike climbed down
again and tried it. "Locked," he said.

"No problem," said Optimus Prime. He lowered
the tail-board at the rear of the truck. "Out you
come, Roller," he said. "I've a feeling there will be
work for you."

Roller, the Autobot scout car, trundled out and onto the road. He ran under the bottom edge of the security fence while Optimus Prime transformed. Upright, he towered above the fence. Reaching down he picked up Spike and his father. Then, with one giant stride he stepped over the fence and into the complex.

In the distance loomed the huge mirrored saucers and the shining metal sphere. A bustle of activity in their shadow showed where the Decepticons were hard at work.

The giant Autobot leader and his human friends
made a wide circle around the edge of the
complex to see what their enemies were up to.
Roller scurried ahead. And then they stopped.
"What can you see from up there?" asked Spike.

"The Decepticons are charging their energon
cubes from that huge sphere over there," replied
Optimus Prime.

"We'd better call up the others," said Spike.

"There isn't time for that," said Optimus Prime. "It looks as though they are almost finished. We must stop them somehow."

"You have energy weapons..." said Spike.

"Yes," replied Optimus Prime. "But I want to avoid a shoot-out. We are only guests here on your planet Earth. The last thing I want is to cause unnecessary damage to this very valuable equipment. We must strike swiftly and suddenly. Most important of all, the energon cubes must be destroyed!"

From the cover of a rocky outcrop, Spike and his father watched the activity of the Decepticons.

The Decepticons worked fast. They had used magnetic clamps to fix their energy conductors to the metal surface of the energy convertor. The conductors carried the solar energy to the empty energon cubes.

A chain of Decepticons stacked the charged cubes some distance away, close to the fence which ran round the complex. There were only a few empty cubes waiting to be filled.

The four enormous mirrored saucers had moved automatically to follow the sun, but the single smaller saucer in the centre still directed its stream of golden energy onto the convertor. Spike turned as his father nudged him. "There's our weapon," he whispered. "I think that the small saucer is on some sort of turntable so that it can be adjusted. If I can get to the building there, I think I'll be able to find the controls." He started to crawl forward.

Spike stopped him. "Let me go, Dad," he said. "I'm smaller. I'm not so likely to be spotted by the Decepticons." And before his father could stop him, Spike was darting from one patch of cover to the next, heading for the building in the centre of the complex.

In a few minutes Spike stood by the wall of the building. Carefully, he crept round to the metal door. Luckily, the Decepticons were working on the other side. Spike gripped the handle but nothing happened. The door was locked. He took out his clasp knife. Perhaps he could pick the lock. No, he needed expert help... and quickly! The Decepticons had finished their task and were now dismantling their gear.

Spike looked up the slope to where his father and Optimus Prime were hidden. Holding his knife so that the sun shone on the blade he began to signal. Optimus Prime saw the flashes first. "What is it?" he said.

Spike's father said, "It's Spike. He's signalling in morse. Something must be wrong." He read off the signal: D – O – O – R L – O – C – K – E – D!

"This will do the trick," said Optimus Prime. "It's a standard piece of Autobot repair equipment. A sonic multi-tool. Come here, Roller."

With a chatter of electronics, Roller trundled up. Optimus Prime took the sonic multi-tool and tucked it into Roller's cargo compartment and sent him speeding down to where Spike waited.

Soundwave was supervising the last of the work over by the stack of energon cubes. Suddenly he paused. Something had caught his attention. There had been a slight movement near the building.

He watched for a moment, but saw nothing else. It was probably one of those strange Earth creatures that seemed to be everywhere on this outlandish planet.

Unaware that Soundwave had caught a glimpse of him moving through the grass, Roller halted at Spike's feet. Spike found the sonar multi-tool and looked at it, puzzled. It didn't look much.

He pressed a switch on the side. Nothing happened. He turned it towards the door... and with a faint click he heard the lock open.

Next minute he was inside.

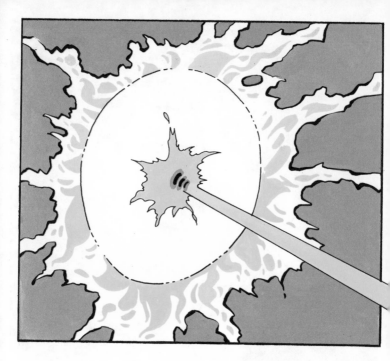

One by one the Decepticons reported to Soundwave. Their equipment and energon cubes were all checked and correct.

Soundwave turned to report to Megatron but stopped, suddenly. His sensors had picked up something this time. Next moment he gave the alarm: "INTRUDER! INTRUDER! DETECT HUMAN INTRUDER!"

Instantly the Decepticons formed a defensive screen around the precious energon cubes and waited. Nothing happened. No shots. No sudden attack.

Then Starscream shouted, "The solar machinery! It's gone mad!" He aimed his null-ray projector at the steadily swinging saucer. But he was too late. The golden solar energy no longer blazed onto the convertor. The beam was aiming straight at the stack of energon cubes. For a moment they pulsed with a million megajoules of super-energy then, in one blinding ball of fire, they disintegrated.

The Decepticons were hurled in all directions, and lay in scattered heaps as the last of their precious energy flickered and died in the scorched earth.

The dazed and battered Decepticons rose
unsteadily to their feet. One by one they took off
and headed back to their base. Megatron was the
last to go. He took a final look at the smoking
energon cubes and saw Optimus Prime striding
down the hill with Spike's father, running hard to
keep up, behind him.

"PRIME!" cried Megatron. "I might have known
that this was your doing. You will regret the day
that you dared to interfere in the affairs of the
Decepticons!"

With a snarl of rage Megatron rose into the air,
to return to his base and hatch more plans for the
defeat of the Autobots and his final triumph on
Cybertron.

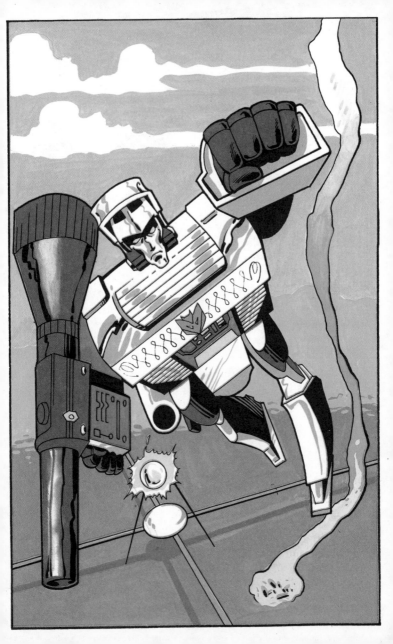

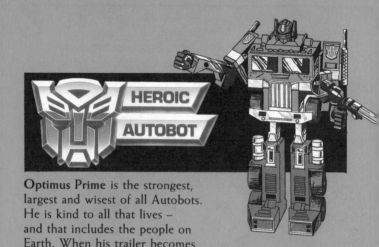

Optimus Prime is the strongest, largest and wisest of all Autobots. He is kind to all that lives – and that includes the people on Earth. When his trailer becomes the command centre, he transforms from the trailer cab to lead the Autobots in their fight against the evil Decepticons.

Hound transforms from a four-wheel-drive vehicle to the Autobot scout robot. He is brave and loyal to the Autobot cause and likes the planet Earth. Secretly, Hound would like to be human!

Sideswipe transforms from a racing car to a warrior robot. He and his twin brother, Sunstreaker, make a powerful team in the never-ending battle against the Decepticons.

Huffer transforms from a trailer cab to become the Autobot construction engineer. Although he will mutter and complain, he is a strong and reliable worker.

Jazz transforms from a racing car to the Autobot special operations agent. He takes on the dangerous missions and is clever and daring. He likes Earth and is always looking to learn more about the planet and its people.

Gears transforms from an armoured carrier to work as a transport and reconnaissance robot. Like Huffer, he likes to be miserable and find fault in everything, but he has great strength and endurance.